STARTING POINTS

# SPRING

### Ruth Thomson

Photography by Peter Millard

**FRANKLIN WATTS**
LONDON · NEW YORK · SYDNEY · TORONTO

Franklin Watts Inc.
387 Park Avenue South
New York, NY 10016

Library of Congress Cataloging-in-Publication Data
Thomson, Ruth.
Spring/Ruth Thomson.
p. cm. — (Starting points)
Summary: Presents a wide variety of projects and activities based on the theme of spring.
ISBN: 0 531 14018-0
1. Spring — Juvenile literature. (1. Spring. 2. Handicraft.)
I. Title. II. Series: Thomson. Ruth. Starting points.
QB637.5.T46 1990
745.5 dc20
89-36534 CIP AC

Editor: Jenny Wood
Design: David Bennett Books Ltd.
Picture research: Sarah Ridley
Rachel Wright
Typesetting: Type City, St Albans
Printed in Belgium

The author and publisher would like to thank Sharon Fuller and
Margaret Howker and children from the Brixton Saturday Explorers'
Club for providing the giant nest; Jack Rollo for his decorated eggs;
Rachel Wright for her papercuts.
Picture credits:-
Heather Angel: Page 28 (top left);
Aquila: Page 7 (top and bottom left);
Survival Anglia: Pages 6 (bottom left), 7 (top and bottom right), 10 (bottom), 11 (top left and top and bottom right);
Chris Fairclough Colour Library: Page 4
Barrie Watts: Pages 6 (bottom right), 26, 27, 28 ( right);
Zefa: Pages 6 (top), 10 (top), 11 (bottom left), 28 (bottom left).

# CONTENTS

Spring is here    4

Signs of spring    6

Tree flowers    8

Busy birds    10

Colored eggs    12

Nests and baskets    18

Paper flowers    20

Woolly sheep    22

Papercuts    24

Frogs and toads    26

Pond watch    28

More things to do    29

A spring quiz    31

Spring words    31

Index    32

# Spring Is Here

*A little bit of blowing,*
*A little bit of snow,*
*A little bit of growing,*
*And the crocuses will show;*
*On every twig that's lonely*
*A new green leaf will spring;*
*On every patient tree-top*
*A thrush will perch and sing.*

*Anon*

# Signs of Spring

As the days grow warmer and longer, plants begin to grow again and animals become more active.

Most farm animals give birth to their young in spring, when there is plenty of lush new grass to feed on.

Violets

Wood anemones

Woodland flowers bloom early, before the leaves of the trees start to grow and shade the woodland floor. As well as anemones and violets, you will find Solomon's seal, Jack-in-the-pulpit and bloodroot.

When the weather becomes warm enough, queen bumble bees wake up and fly around looking for a suitable place to build a nest.

Butterflies that have survived the winter fly around on sunny days, feeding on the nectar of spring flowers.

Thrush

Great crested grebes

Noisy signs of spring are male birds, who sing to attract females. Once a bird has chosen a mate, they build a nest together. The male bird sings all day to warn other birds away from its site.

Birds which do not have good voices use other ways to attract a mate, either with a flying display or by showing off their fine feathers. Some birds perform a courtship dance. Sometimes the females dance as well.

# Tree Flowers

In spring, sap rises up the trees and feeds the buds, which swell. The buds open to reveal leaves and flowers.

▲ Maple spike
(insect-pollinated)

▲ Willow Catkins
(wind-pollinated)

All trees have flowers. These produce fruits and seeds from which new trees can grow. Each flower has male parts called stamens, which hold tiny grains of pollen. The female part of the flower is called an ovary and holds ovules. When pollen reaches the ovules, they join and the ovules start to grow into seeds.

The pollen is carried to the ovules either by insects or by the wind. Many tree flowers have brightly-colored, scented flowers to attract insects.

◄ Walnut Catkins
(Wind-pollinated)

Beech Flowers
(wind-pollinated) ▶

◄
Birch
Catkins
(wind-
pollinated)

## ▲ Ornamental Cherry

As an insect feeds on the sweet liquid, called nectar, inside a flower, its body is dusted with pollen, which it brushes on to the next flower it visits.

Trees which are pollinated by the wind have small, dull flowers with no petals or nectar. The male and female flowers grow separately in long clusters called catkins. The wind blows the pollen from the male catkins on to the female ones.

▶ Rowan Flowers (insect-pollinated)

◀ Hawthorn Flowers (insect-pollinated)

◀ Apple Flowers (insect-pollinated)

◀ Horse Chestnut (pollinated by bees)

# Busy Birds

Birds are busy all spring, building their nests, laying their eggs and feeding their young.

Each species of bird builds a distinctively shaped nest on a particular kind of site. The nests are mostly well hidden or built in inaccessible places, so that the eggs are well protected.

Some birds make nests in a shallow hollow in the ground. They lay speckled eggs which blend in with their surroundings. Waterbirds often make a nest of heaped waterplants on the surface of shallow water. Many seabirds build nests on rocks or on cliff ledges. Woodland birds often build nests in dense bushes or in tree hollows.

Nests are made of all sorts of materials. Swallows make theirs of mud and straw; goldfinches use grass, moss and plant down; thrushes build nests of twigs, earth, grass and moss. Usually, nests have a soft lining of feathers or hair, which helps to keep the eggs warm.

Starlings nest in holes in trees.

Grebes make nests of waterplants anchored in shallow water.

Crow

Arctic Loon turning its eggs.

Crows make untidy nests of twigs in tall trees. They nest close to one another.

The birds sit on their eggs to keep them warm until they hatch. They turn them from time to time to make sure they stay at an even temperature all over.

Thrush

Ptarmigan chick

Baby birds that hatch in nests are naked and blind. They cannot feed themselves and have no feathers for flying. Their parents spend all day gathering food for them to eat.

Baby birds that are born on the ground are covered with down feathers, which keep them warm. The down is often mottled, which makes the baby birds difficult to see.

# Colored Eggs

Giving colored eggs is a very ancient tradition which celebrates the rebirth of nature in spring

## Preparing the eggs

Before you color eggs, you must either hard-boil or blow them. First, keep them at room temperature overnight.

If you want to boil eggs, start them in a saucepan of cold water. When the water comes to the boil, turn down the heat immediately and allow the eggs to simmer gently. This will help prevent them from cracking. If you want to keep, and not eat, the eggs, simmer them for at least half an hour.

## Blowing eggs

If you want to keep your eggs as ornaments, it is best to blow them. They will then keep for as long as you like and you can use the insides for cooking.

Prick a hole in the wider end with a darning needle. Wiggle it about to make the hole bigger, and break away tiny bits of shell. Turn the egg over and gently prick a hole in the pointed end. Do not make this hole any bigger.

Cover the two holes with your finger and thumb and gently shake the egg to break up the yolk inside.

Hold the egg over a bowl and blow through the hole at the pointed end. You will need to blow quite hard. The contents will empty into the bowl. If they get stuck, shake the egg again.

Clean the egg thoroughly by holding it with the bigger hole uppermost under a running tap. Blow the water out through the small hole and shake the egg dry.

# Dyed eggs

Edible food colors and cold-water fabric dyes give strong, bright colors. Use food colors straight from the bottle or dilute them with water. Mix fabric dyes according to their instructions. If you want to eat the eggs, use only edible food dyes and eat them within three days.

If you prefer softer colors, make some natural dyes instead. Try using these ingredients, or experiment with others, such as carrots, coffee and spinach. Boil the ingredients in a pan of water, with a tablespoon of vinegar added, until the water strongly changes color.

Turn off the heat and put the eggs into the dye. Leave them overnight. Take them out and let them dry, then gently rub them with a tissue dipped in cooking oil to deepen the color.

Food colouring

Fabric dyes

Onion skins

Turmeric

Beet

Apple skins

Red Cabbage

13

# Marbled eggs

These are two ways to marble eggs.

1. Surround an egg with the outer skins of several onions.
2. Wrap a square of cotton over the skins to keep them in place. Secure the cotton with rubber bands.
3. Hard-boil the egg for half an hour and leave it to cool completely before unwrapping.

1. Crack the shell of a hard-boiled egg all over with a knife blade. With the point of the knife, remove little pieces of shell here and there.

2. Spoon the egg into a pan of edible dye and let it boil for 10 minutes or so. When the egg is cool, peel off the shell to reveal the marbling.

# Patterned eggs

You can also use dyes to make decorative patterned eggs.

▲
Collect a few pretty leaves. Dip one in some salad oil and lay it on the shell of a boiled egg. Wrap the egg in a piece of nylon cut from a pair of old tights or panty hose. Tie it tightly so that dye cannot seep under the leaf. Leave the egg to soak in the dye. Do not remove the nylon until the dye has dried.

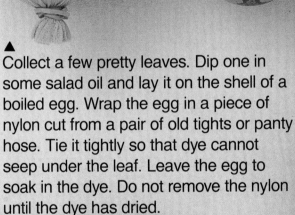

▲
Draw a pattern on the shell of a hard-boiled egg with wax crayons. Fat lines show up the best. Dye the egg and put it on crumpled aluminum foil to dry. The dye will not have taken where the wax crayon marks are.

▲
Dye a hard-boiled egg a deep color and dry it. With the point of a knife scratch a design in the dye.

# Decorated eggs

These are some of the hundreds of ways to decorate eggs. If you want to make a symmetrical pattern, draw pencil lines around the egg as a guide.

▲Felt-tip pens▼

Sequins
▼

Ribbons
▼

Shells
▼

Stick on all sorts of odds and ends with Elmer's glue, to create special effects.

Tissue paper and dried flowers▶

▶
Sticky
paper shapes

Glue on overlapping pieces of tissue paper. A coat of paper varnish gives a shiny finish. ▶

**Glass paint** ▶
▼

▶ To hang up a blown egg, tie a length of thread around a spent match, and push the match into the larger of the two holes.

You can use almost any sort of paint to decorate eggs.

Write a message on a ▲ dyed egg with dry transfer letters.

**Fabric dye and acrylic** ▲

**Water color** ▲
◀

**Ready-mixed poster paint and varnish** ▶

**Gouache** ▲

**Batik and Sticky Shapes** ▶

**Batik** ▼

x pattern

**Batik** ▶

Batik eggs are waxed and dyed. Drip candle wax on to an egg in a pattern. When it hardens, dip the egg in a light-colored dye. Dry it. Repeat the waxing and dyeing with a darker color.

17

# Nests and Baskets

Once you have colored your eggs, make some nests or decorate little baskets to present them in.

## Raffia nest

To make the base, tie a loose circle of raffia around the rim of a bowl. Circle the raffia several more times and weave it in and out through the circles. Then weave across the base of the bowl until you have a fairly sturdy shape. Carefully lift the nest off the bowl and continue weaving upwards.

## Grass nest

Braid some long blades of grass. Shape the braids around and around on top of one another, to make a nest shape. Bind them together with single grass blades. Line the nest with moss.

## Decorated baskets

Line ready-made baskets with tissue paper, felt and cotton wool, or use natural materials such as leaves, grass, raffia or moss.

Twist ribbons round the handles and poke flowers or leaves into the sides. You might like to attach a gift tag (see page 25 for ideas).

# Decorated container

A clear plastic food container, covered with wrapping paper and decorated, makes a very effective nest. Line it with shredded tissue paper or raffia.

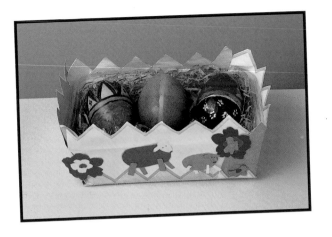

These children made an enormous nest by weaving bendy willow twigs through a wicker frame. The nest was decorated with spring flowers and lined with feathers from pillows.

# Paper Flowers

Leave spring flowers in woods and gardens for everyone to enjoy. Instead, make some paper ones of your own.

## Things you need:
- **Crepe and tissue paper**
- **Pipe cleaners**
- **Scissors**
- **Ruler**
- **Pencil**
- **Glue**
- **Thread**

## Crepe paper daffodils

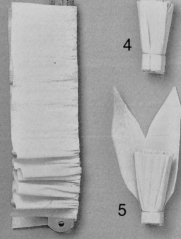

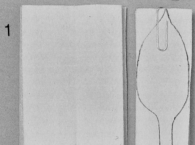

1. Cut two rectangles of yellow paper, 9 inches by 4 inches (24cm by 10cm), with the grain parallel to the short end. Fold one of them into six pleats.

2. Draw a petal shape on the top pleat and cut it out through all six pleats.

3. Fold the other pleat in half lengthwise. Put a ruler in the fold and ruffle the paper along it.

4. Roll up the ruffled paper. Hold the folded edge in your mouth and tie the other end with thread.

5. Glue three petals around the base of the roll. Glue the other three on top of them.

6. Glue a length of green paper around a pipe cleaner to make the stem.

7. Push the end of the pipe cleaner into the center of the flower. Cover the join between the base of the flower and the top of the stem with a small rectangle of green paper.

8. When the glue has completely dried, bend the petals outwards.

Daffodils

Primroses

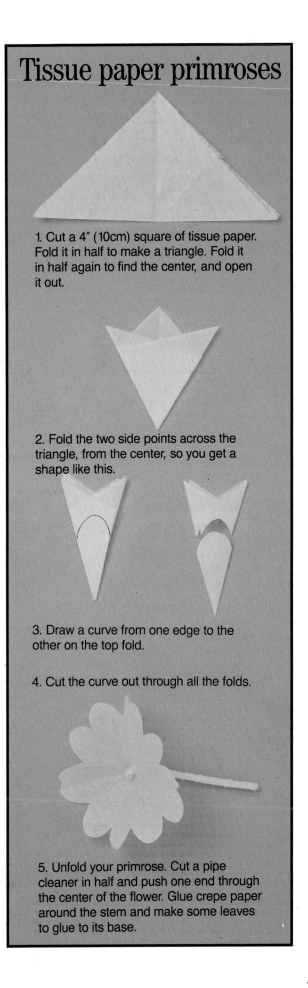

# Tissue paper primroses

1. Cut a 4″ (10cm) square of tissue paper. Fold it in half to make a triangle. Fold it in half again to find the center, and open it out.

2. Fold the two side points across the triangle, from the center, so you get a shape like this.

3. Draw a curve from one edge to the other on the top fold.

4. Cut the curve out through all the folds.

5. Unfold your primrose. Cut a pipe cleaner in half and push one end through the center of the flower. Glue crepe paper around the stem and make some leaves to glue to its base.

# Woolly Sheep

Sheep are shorn of their winter fleeces soon after lambing. Collect wool caught on bushes or fences and make some woolly sheep of your own.

It is best to wash the wool first in warm, soapy water, picking out any bits and pieces. When it is dry, pull the fibers apart.

## Greetings cards

Fold a piece of stiff paper or cardboard in half to make a card shape. Glue some wool in the center, then draw a sheep's head and legs, and some grass. Of course, you can make all sorts of animals other than sheep — use the wool to make a fluffy rabbit's tail or a furry cat, for example.

# Sheep brooch

## Things you need:

- **Wool**
- **Three pipe cleaners**
- **A safety pin**

1. Make a sheep's head with one of the pipe cleaners. Bend the other two into pairs of legs, leaving some of the length.

2. Twist the three pipe cleaners together to make a sheep skeleton.

3. Roll some wool between your palms to make a long strand. Wind it around the skeleton and tuck in the end.

4. Attach a safety pin on one side, so you can use your sheep as a brooch.

1

2

3

4

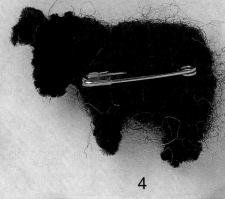

# Papercuts

Make some brightly-colored cut paper designs, inspired by sights you see in spring. In Poland, people used to decorate their homes with these.

## Things you need:

- **An assortment of brightly colored paper**
- **A pencil**
- **A pair of small scissors with sharp points**
- **Masking tape**
- **Glue**

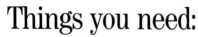

Fold a piece of paper in half. Press your thumb along the crease. Fix the open sides together with masking tape. Draw half your design on one side of the paper, using the fold as the center line. At this stage make the outline bold and simple.

Cut out your design. If you want to add more detail, cut small notches around the edges and glue on offcuts, in contrasting colors, from other cut paper.

You can use
cut paper designs
to decorate cards
or gift tags.
Try making a
collage of
several designs.

## Tips and wrinkles

* Always cut the patterns on the fold first.
* If you want to make cuts in the middle of the paper, make a hole first, by pressing one scissor point through the paper onto some modeling clay.
* Remember to leave small, bridging pieces of paper to hold your design together. Be careful not to cut away the whole fold.

# Frogs and Toads

In spring, frogs and toads emerge from hibernation and gather in ponds and ditches to breed. You will hear the males croaking.

Frog

Toad

It is easy to tell frogs and toads apart. Frogs have smooth, moist skin and hop or jump about on long back legs. Toads have dry, warty skin and move by crawling on short legs.

Frogs mating in water

Frogspawn

Toadspawn

Their spawn (eggs) is quite different as well. Frogs lay up to 3,000 eggs in a clump. They are protected by a jelly coating, which absorbs water. This enables the spawn to float on the surface of the pond in the warmth.

Toads lay eggs in a continuous strand of jelly, which can be as long as 10 feet (3m), and contain over 2,000 eggs. The strand twines around water weed beneath the pond's surface.

Frog tadpoles emerge from the jelly after about two weeks, and cling to its surface. At first they breathe through feathery, external gills, which are absorbed after four weeks or so.

Soon the tadpoles start eating algae and shelter among the weeds. Hundreds of them are eaten by fish, insects and newts. At about seven weeks, hind legs appear.

As the tadpoles grow older, they start to feed on small pond animals. By twelve weeks, their front legs appear and their tail starts to shrink.

Young frogs leave the pond in June or July and spend the summer in long, damp grass. A frog feeds on insects, which it catches with its long, sticky tongue.

# Pond Watch

As the days get warmer, ponds start teeming with life.

## An underwater viewer

Remove the top and bottom of a large can. Tape the sharp edges. Stretch a piece of transparent plastic wrap over one end and hold it in place with a rubber band. Dip the viewer in water, and the pressure will push up the plastic giving you a magnified view.

▲ Pond skaters skim across the surface, feeding on dead insects, which they grasp with their short front legs.

▲ Newts live on land. In spring, they move to water to breed. The male newt is normally brown. In the breeding season, it develops a crest on its back and spots all over its body. The male courts a female by waving its tail very rapidly in front of her.

◀ The backswimmer spends most of its time hanging just below the water's surface. It feeds on small fish, tadpoles and insects. It swims on its back, using its powerful back legs.

# More Things To Do

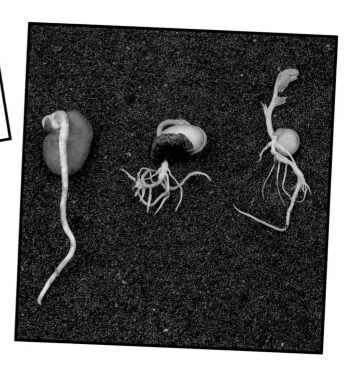

## Planting seeds

When the sun starts to warm up the ground, it is time to sow seeds. If you have a garden, try growing some vegetables of your own. Follow the instructions on the seed packets.

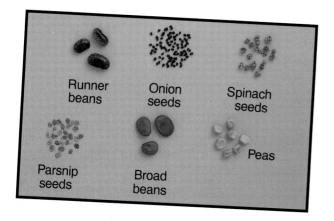

Runner beans

Onion seeds

Spinach seeds

Parsnip seeds

Broad beans

Peas

If you want to see how seeds start growing, soak lots of peas and beans overnight and then plant them in several different pots in some potting compost. Label them with their name and the date you sowed them. Keep the soil moist.

After three days, dig up one of the seeds to see how the roots are developing. Keep a record with drawings of what you find. Dig up another seed every day, until the shoot appears. Then record how many leaves appear and when they come out.

This broad bean, scarlet bean and pea were all planted at the same time. Compare how they have grown in just over a week.

## Bird territories

At nesting time, some birds, such as robins, thrushes and blackbirds defend their nest area, or territory, by singing in the same places every day. These places often mark the edges of their territory.

Try to discover the extent of birds' territories by mapping your garden, or an area you often visit. Draw the map accurately, on graph paper. Mark in the position of the main trees, shrubs and bushes, and any posts where you see birds perch.

Observe the birds at the same time each day (the early morning is often best), and mark their singing perches on your map.

# Tree watch

The time trees come into leaf and flower differs considerably. Some trees produce leaves before their flowers; the flowers of others appear well before their leaves; some trees have leaves and flowers at the same time.

Keep a record, like the one below, of the trees in your garden or in a nearby area. Discover what differences there are between trees whose flowers are wind-pollinated and those which are pollinated by insects.

| Tree | Leaves appear first | Flowers appear first | Flowers & Leaves appear together | Wind - pollinated | Insect- pollinated |
|---|---|---|---|---|---|
| Ash | | | | | |
| Beech | | | | | |
| Birch | | | | | |
| Cherry | | | | | |
| Hawthorn | | | | | |
| Hazel | | ✓ | | ✓ | |
| Horse Chestnut | | | | | |
| Maple | | | ✓ | | ✓ |
| Mountain Ash | | | | | |
| Sloe | | | | | |
| Willow | | | | | |

# Keeping tadpoles

If you want to watch tadpoles, collect a small number of frog eggs (never a big clump), in a jar of pond water. Collect some waterweed for the tadpoles to feed on, as well.

Line the bottom of a big aquarium with a layer of gravel, covered with some well-washed sand. Anchor the pondweed under some big stones.

Fill the aquarium with tap water and allow it to stand overnight before you put in the frogs eggs. If possible, add some pond water as well.

Newly-hatched tadpoles will cling to and feed on the waterweed. After a few days, give them small amounts of shredded lettuce. A week or so later, sprinkle small amounts of flaked fish food at intervals.

Release the tadpoles by the edge of a pond, once their back legs are fully formed.

# Nesting materials

Hang up some wool, torn tissue paper, raffia and feathers from a branch. Keep a watch to see what birds come to collect these different materials for making their nests.

# A spring quiz

If you get stuck, you will find some clues by looking back through the book. The answers are on page 32.

1. Which of these birds does *not* build a nest of its own?
   a) sparrow  b) thrush  c) robin
   d) cuckoo  e) blackbird  f) crow

2. Which of these insects is the odd one out?
   a) dragonfly  b) mosquito
   c) mayfly  d) ladybug  e) gnat

3. How many eggs does a frog lay at one time?
   a) about 30  b) about 300
   c) about 3,000  d) about 30,000

4. Which of these spring flowers grow from bulbs?
   a) bluebell  b) wood anemone
   c) tulip  d) daffodil  e) primrose

5. Which of these tree flowers are pollinated by the wind?
   a) cherry  b) hazel  c) birch
   d) alder  e) horse chestnut

6. Which part of a plant grows first from a seed?
   a) the roots  b) the leaves
   c) the shoot

7. True or false?
   a) Frogs breathe through their skin.
   b) Toads do not hop, they crawl.
   c) Frogs live in water all year around.
   d) Frogs can change color to match their surroundings.
   e) Toads lay their eggs in a continuous strand of jelly.
   f) Frogs have webbed feet.
   g) Frog and toad eggs are called spawn.

# Spring words

How would you describe spring? Think about the colors, atmosphere, sights, weather and your feelings. Here are some words to start you thinking.

| Weather | Animals, birds and insects | | Plants | |
|---|---|---|---|---|
| breezy | emerge | flutter | seeds | sap |
| blowing | frisky | scatter | burst | petal |
| blustery | gambol | burst | bud | scales |
| showery | fluffy | fleecy | germinate | shoot |
| squally | furry | swarm | sow | pollen |
| damp | chirp | hatch | bloom | bough |
| bright | cheep | dabble | blossom | swell |
| changeable | broody | cluster | catkin | scented |
| rainbows | nesting | settle | tufted | posy |
| moist | spawn | egg | fresh | |

# Index

Alder 31
Apple 9
Aquarium 30
Arctic Loon 11

Basket 18, 19
Beech 8
Birch 8, 31
Birds 5, 7, 10, 29, 31
Blackbird 29, 31
Bluebells 31
Bloodroot 6
Brooch 23
Bud 8
Bulb 31
Bumblebee 7
Butterflies 7

Catkins 8, 9
Courtship 7
Crocus 5
Crow 11, 31
Cuckoo 31
Cut paper designs 24, 25

Daffodils 20, 31
Dragonfly 31
Dyes 13, 14, 15
  Fabric dyes 13
  Food dyes 13
  Natural dyes 13

Eggs 10, 11, 12, 13, 14, 15, 16, 17
  Batik eggs 17
  Birds' eggs 10, 11
  Blown eggs 12, 16, 17
  Boiled eggs 12, 13, 14, 15
  Decorated eggs 16, 17
  Dyed eggs 13, 14, 15, 17
  Hanging eggs 17

Marbled eggs 14
Painted eggs 17
Patterned eggs 15

Farm animals 6
Feather 10, 11, 19, 30
Fish 27
Fleece 22
Flowers 6, 8, 19, 30
Frogs 26, 27, 31
Fruits 8

Gift tags 19, 25
Gills 27
Gnat 31
Goldfinch 10
Grass 18, 19, 22, 27
Grebe 7, 10
Greetings cards 22, 25

Hawthorn 9
Hazel 31
Hibernation 26
Horse chestnut 9, 31

Insect pollination 9, 30
Insects 8, 9, 27, 28, 30

Jack-in-the-pulpit 6

Ladybug 31
Leaves 8, 15, 17, 19, 30

Mosquito 31
Moss 18, 19

Nectar 7, 9
Nest 6, 7, 10, 18, 19, 30
Newt 27, 28

Ornamental cherry 9, 31
Ovary 8
Ovule 8

Paper 16, 19, 20, 21, 24, 25, 30
Paper flowers 20, 21
Petals 9, 20
Pollen 8, 9
Pollination 9, 30
Pond 26, 27, 28
Pond skater 28
Primrose 21, 31
Ptarmigan 11

Raffia 18, 19, 30
Robin 29, 31
Rowan 9

Sap 8
Seeds 8, 29, 31
Sheep 22, 23
Solomon's seal 6
Sparrow 31
Spawn 26, 31
Stamen 8
Starling 10
Swallow 10
Sycamore 8

Tadpole 27, 30
Thrush 5, 7, 10, 11, 29, 31
Toad 26, 31
Trees 8, 30
Tulip 31

Underwater viewer 29

Vegetables 29
Violets 6

Walnut 8
Water boatman 28
Willow, 8, 19
Wind pollination 8, 30
Wood anemone 6, 31
Wool 22, 23, 30

# Answers to the spring quiz

1d A cuckoo does not build a nest of its own.

2e The ladybug is the odd one out. It is the only insect whose larvae do not hatch and live in water.

3c A frog lays about 3,000 eggs at a time.

4a,c,d Bluebells, tulips and daffodils grow from bulbs.

5b,c,d Hazel, birch and alder flowers are pollinated by the wind.

6a The roots of a plant grow first.

7a,b,d,e,f,g True. 7c False.